BASICS OF CRYPTO STAKING

PART OF OUR SERIES:

TOMORROW'S TECH: UNDERSTANDING THE BASICS

LIMITLESS PUBLISHING @ 2024

Table of Contents

Chapter 1: Introduction to Staking of Cryptocurrencies 1
- Overview of staking as a method of validating transactions in blockchain networks 1
- Explanation of the concept of staking in the context of cryptocurrency 3
- Historical background and evolution of staking in the crypto space 4

Chapter 2: How Staking Works 6
- Detailed explanation of the staking process in cryptocurrency 6
- Comparison between proof-of-work (PoW) and proof-of-stake (PoS) consensus algorithms 7
- Role of stakers in securing the network and validating transactions 9

Chapter 3: Choosing the Right Staking Cryptocurrency 11
- Factors to consider when selecting a cryptocurrency for staking 11
- Comparison of popular staking coins and their rewards mechanisms 13
- Risks and benefits associated with staking different cryptocurrencies 15

Chapter 4: Setting Up a Staking Wallet 17
- Guide on how to set up a staking wallet for storing and managing staked coins 17
- Overview of different types of staking wallets (Online, Hardware, Software) 19
- Security best practices for protecting staked assets 21

Chapter 5: Staking Strategies and Tips 23
- Different staking strategies to maximize returns and minimize risks 23
- Tips for successful staking, including timing, network participation, and diversification . 24
- Overview of tools and resources available for stakers to monitor and optimize their staking activities 26

Chapter 6: Staking Pool Participation 29
- Explanation of staking pools and how they work 29
- Pros and cons of joining a staking pool versus staking independently 30
- Steps to participate in a staking pool and earn rewards collaboratively 33

Conclusion 34
- Recap of key concepts covered in the book 34
- Future trends and developments in the staking ecosystem 36
- Final thoughts on the importance of staking in the broader cryptocurrency landscape 38

Chapter 1: Introduction to Staking of Cryptocurrencies

- Overview of staking as a method of validating transactions in blockchain networks

Staking has emerged as a popular method for validating transactions in blockchain networks, providing an alternative to the traditional proof-of-work consensus mechanism. In this section, we will delve into the basics of staking, how it works, its benefits, and its role in securing blockchain networks.

Introduction to Staking

Staking is a consensus mechanism used in blockchain networks to secure the network and validate transactions. Instead of relying on miners to solve complex mathematical puzzles as in proof-of-work systems, staking involves participants, known as validators, locking up a certain amount of cryptocurrency as collateral to participate in the validation process.

How Staking Works

Validators in a staking network are chosen to create new blocks and validate transactions based on the amount of cryptocurrency they hold and are willing to "stake." The higher the stake, the higher the chances of being selected to validate transactions and receive rewards in the form of newly minted coins or transaction fees.

Validators are required to follow the rules of the network and are financially incentivized to act honestly, as any malicious behavior could result in penalties, including losing their staked coins.

Benefits of Staking

1. Energy Efficiency: Staking is more energy-efficient compared to proof-of-work systems, as it does not require vast amounts of computational power to validate transactions.

2. Security: Staking enhances the security of blockchain networks, as validators have a financial stake in the network's integrity and are incentivized to follow the rules.

3. Decentralization: Staking promotes decentralization by allowing anyone to participate in the validation process, as long as they hold the required amount of cryptocurrency.

4. Passive Income: Staking offers participants the opportunity to earn passive income by staking their cryptocurrency and validating transactions.

Role in Securing Blockchain Networks

Staking plays a crucial role in securing blockchain networks by ensuring that transactions are validated efficiently and securely. Validators are responsible for creating new blocks, adding transactions to the blockchain, and reaching consensus on the state of the network.

By participating in staking, individuals contribute to the overall security and decentralization of the network, helping to maintain its integrity and reliability.

In conclusion, staking is a fundamental aspect of blockchain technology that provides an alternative method for validating transactions and securing networks. It offers numerous benefits, including energy efficiency, security, decentralization, and the opportunity for participants to earn passive income through staking their cryptocurrency.

- Explanation of the concept of staking in the context of cryptocurrency

Staking is a fundamental concept in the world of cryptocurrencies that plays a crucial role in securing blockchain networks and validating transactions. In simple terms, staking involves participating in the process of securing a blockchain network by holding and locking up a certain amount of cryptocurrency tokens in a wallet. In return for staking these tokens, participants are rewarded with additional tokens as an incentive for helping to maintain the network's integrity.

The process of staking is often compared to mining in traditional proof-of-work blockchain systems like Bitcoin. However, in staking, there is no need for powerful computational resources to solve complex mathematical puzzles. Instead, validators are chosen to create new blocks and validate transactions based on the number of tokens they hold and are willing to stake.

Staking is made possible by the underlying consensus mechanism of a blockchain network, with Proof of Stake (PoS) being one of the most popular methods. In a PoS system, validators are selected to create new blocks and validate transactions based on the number of tokens they hold and are willing to lock up as collateral. This mechanism is designed to encourage network participants to act honestly and in the best interest of the network, as they have a financial stake in maintaining its security and integrity.

By staking their tokens, participants help secure the network, reduce the risk of attacks, and ensure the smooth operation of the blockchain. In return, they earn staking rewards, which can be in the form of additional tokens, transaction fees, or other benefits defined by the network protocol.

Staking has become increasingly popular in the cryptocurrency space as more blockchain projects transition from traditional proof-of-work to proof-of-stake consensus mechanisms. It offers an environmentally friendly alternative to energy-intensive mining operations and provides an opportunity for token holders to earn passive income by actively participating in the network.

Overall, staking is a key concept in the world of cryptocurrencies that incentivizes active participation in blockchain networks, promotes network security, and rewards users for contributing to the ecosystem's growth and sustainability.

- Historical background and evolution of staking in the crypto space

Staking, also known as Proof of Stake (PoS), is a consensus algorithm used in blockchain networks to secure the network and validate transactions. The concept of staking dates back to the early days of cryptocurrencies, with the first implementation being introduced by Peercoin in 2012. Peercoin was one of the first cryptocurrencies to use a PoS algorithm as an alternative to the energy-intensive Proof of Work (PoW) algorithm used by Bitcoin.

Over the years, staking has gained popularity in the crypto space due to its energy efficiency and potential for decentralization. As more projects started adopting PoS algorithms, staking became a common practice for investors and users to earn rewards by participating in network validation.

One of the key milestones in the evolution of staking was the introduction of delegated staking, where users can delegate their coins to a validator node to participate in network consensus without the need for technical expertise or a large amount of coins. This innovation made staking more accessible to a wider audience and further contributed to the decentralization of blockchain networks.

Another significant development in the staking space was the emergence of staking pools, which allow users to pool their resources together to increase their chances of being chosen as a validator and sharing the rewards. Staking pools have become a popular way for small investors to participate in staking and earn rewards without the need for a large amount of capital.

As the staking ecosystem continues to evolve, new advancements such as slashing protection mechanisms, cross-chain staking, and innovative staking derivatives are being introduced to improve the security and efficiency of staking networks. With the growing interest in staking and the potential for passive income, staking has become an integral part of the cryptocurrency ecosystem, shaping the future of blockchain technology.

Chapter 2: How Staking Works

- Detailed explanation of the staking process in cryptocurrency

Staking is a process in which cryptocurrency holders participate in the validation and confirmation of transactions on a blockchain network. This process is essential for maintaining the network's security, integrity, and functionality. Here is a detailed explanation of how staking works in the world of cryptocurrency:

1. Proof of Stake (PoS) Consensus Mechanism: Staking is based on the Proof of Stake (PoS) consensus mechanism, which is an alternative to the traditional Proof of Work (PoW) mechanism used in cryptocurrencies like Bitcoin. In PoS, validators are chosen to create new blocks and validate transactions based on the number of coins they hold and are willing to lock up as collateral.

2. Wallet Setup: To participate in staking, cryptocurrency holders need to set up a compatible wallet that supports staking. These wallets are specifically designed to interact with the blockchain network and allow users to stake their coins securely.

3. Locking up Funds: Staking requires participants to lock up a certain amount of cryptocurrency coins as a stake. This stake acts as collateral and incentivizes validators to act honestly and secure the network. The more coins a user stakes, the higher the chances of being chosen as a validator to create new blocks.

4. Block Validation: Validators play a crucial role in the staking process by validating transactions, creating new blocks, and adding them to the blockchain. Validators are selected randomly based on various factors, including the size of their stake and the duration they have been staking.

5. Earning Rewards: In return for their participation in the staking process,

validators earn rewards in the form of additional cryptocurrency coins. These rewards are distributed based on the validator's stake and the network's staking rules. By staking their coins, holders can earn passive income and contribute to the network's security.

6. Network Security: Staking helps secure the network by incentivizing participants to act honestly and follow the consensus rules. Validators are financially motivated to maintain the integrity of the blockchain and prevent malicious actors from disrupting the network.

7. Unstaking and Withdrawal: Staked coins are typically locked up for a certain period, known as the unstaking period. During this period, validators cannot withdraw or transfer their staked coins. Once the unstaking period is over, validators can withdraw their staked coins along with any rewards they have earned.

In conclusion, staking is a fundamental process in the world of cryptocurrency that allows holders to participate in network validation, earn rewards, and contribute to network security. By understanding the staking process and actively participating in it, cryptocurrency holders can engage with their favorite blockchain projects and potentially generate passive income in the form of staking rewards.

- Comparison between proof-of-work (PoW) and proof-of-stake (PoS) consensus algorithms

Cryptocurrencies rely on consensus algorithms to validate transactions and secure the network. Proof-of-Work (PoW) and Proof-of-Stake (PoS) are two prominent consensus mechanisms used in blockchain technology. This section will delve into the key differences and similarities between PoW and PoS.

1. Resource Consumption:
   - PoW: PoW requires miners to solve complex mathematical puzzles to validate transactions. This process demands significant computational power and energy consumption. Miners compete to find the correct hash, leading to high electricity costs and environmental concerns.
   - PoS: In contrast, PoS does not rely on miners solving puzzles. Validators are chosen to create new blocks based on the amount of cryptocurrency they hold and are willing to "stake" as collateral. This eliminates the need for intensive computational resources, making PoS more energy-efficient compared to PoW.

2. Security:
   - PoW: PoW is renowned for its robust security due to the computational work required to solve puzzles. The network is secured by the cumulative computational power of miners, making it resistant to attacks.
   - PoS: PoS relies on the economic incentive of validators to act honestly. Validators are required to stake their own cryptocurrency as collateral, which can be forfeited in case of malicious behavior. While PoS is considered secure, critics argue that it may be vulnerable to attacks if a single entity amasses a majority of the coins.

3. Decentralization:
   - PoW: PoW is often praised for its decentralized nature as anyone with the required hardware can participate in mining. This leads to a distributed network with no single point of control.
   - PoS: PoS can be perceived as less decentralized since block validation is based on the amount of cryptocurrency held. This could potentially concentrate power in the hands of a few large stakeholders, although some PoS implementations employ mechanisms to prevent centralization.

4. Scalability:
   - PoW: The scalability of PoW networks is often limited by the block size and the time it takes to validate transactions through mining. This can lead to

congestion during periods of high activity.
   - PoS: PoS is generally considered more scalable than PoW due to its faster block validation times and lower resource requirements. This allows PoS networks to handle more transactions per second, potentially improving overall scalability.

In conclusion, both PoW and PoS have their own strengths and weaknesses. PoW is known for its security and decentralization, albeit at the cost of high energy consumption. On the other hand, PoS offers a more energy-efficient alternative with potential scalability benefits, although concerns about centralization remain. Understanding the nuances of these consensus algorithms is crucial for anyone interested in the staking of cryptocurrencies.

- **Role of stakers in securing the network and validating transactions**

Stakers play a crucial role in securing the network of a cryptocurrency and validating transactions. Staking is a consensus mechanism in which users lock up a certain amount of their cryptocurrency holdings as collateral to participate in the network's operations. By staking their coins, users are able to actively contribute to the security and integrity of the network in several ways:

1. Block Validation: Stakers are responsible for validating transactions and creating new blocks on the blockchain. When a new transaction is submitted to the network, stakers verify its authenticity and ensure that it complies with the rules of the network. Once validated, the transaction is added to a new block, which is then added to the blockchain.

2. Network Security: Stakers help to secure the network by participating in the block validation process. By staking their coins as collateral, stakers have a financial incentive to act honestly and follow the rules of the network. This helps to prevent malicious actors from attempting to manipulate the blockchain for

personal gain.

3. Consensus Mechanism: Stakers contribute to the consensus mechanism of the network by agreeing on the validity of transactions and reaching consensus on the state of the blockchain. This agreement is crucial for maintaining the integrity and immutability of the blockchain, ensuring that all transactions are recorded accurately and cannot be tampered with.

4. Reward Distribution: In return for their participation in securing the network and validating transactions, stakers are rewarded with additional cryptocurrency coins. These rewards incentivize stakers to continue supporting the network and contribute to its security and decentralization.

5. Decentralization: Stakers help to decentralize the network by distributing the power to validate transactions and create new blocks among a larger group of users. This reduces the risk of a single entity gaining control over the network and helps to maintain its resilience and censorship resistance.

In conclusion, stakers play a vital role in securing the network and validating transactions in a cryptocurrency ecosystem. Their active participation helps to maintain the integrity, security, and decentralization of the network, ensuring that it remains reliable and trustworthy for all users.

Chapter 3: Choosing the Right Staking Cryptocurrency

- Factors to consider when selecting a cryptocurrency for staking

Staking has become a popular method for cryptocurrency investors to earn passive income by participating in the validation of blockchain transactions. When selecting a cryptocurrency for staking, there are several important factors to consider to maximize your returns and minimize risks. Here are some key factors to keep in mind:

1. Staking Rewards: One of the primary considerations when selecting a cryptocurrency for staking is the potential staking rewards. Different cryptocurrencies offer varying annual percentage yields (APY) for staking, so it is important to research and compare the potential returns of different staking coins before making a decision.

2. Staking Requirements: Each cryptocurrency may have specific staking requirements, such as minimum staking amounts, lock-up periods, and technical requirements for running a staking node. It is essential to understand and be comfortable with these requirements before committing to staking a particular cryptocurrency.

3. Security and Reliability: When staking a cryptocurrency, you are essentially entrusting your funds to the network for validation. Therefore, it is crucial to choose a cryptocurrency with a proven track record of security and reliability to minimize the risk of losing your staked assets due to hacks or network failures.

4. Community and Development Team: The strength of the cryptocurrency's community and development team can have a significant impact on the project's long-term success. Look for cryptocurrencies with active communities, transparent development teams, and a clear roadmap for future development

when selecting a coin for staking.

5. Liquidity and Market Cap: Liquidity is an important factor to consider when staking a cryptocurrency, as it determines how easily you can buy or sell your staked coins. It is advisable to choose cryptocurrencies with high liquidity and a substantial market capitalization to ensure that you can easily enter and exit your staking positions.

6. Network Consensus Mechanism: Different cryptocurrencies use various consensus mechanisms for validating transactions, such as Proof of Stake (PoS), Delegated Proof of Stake (DPoS), or Proof of Authority (PoA). Understanding the consensus mechanism of a cryptocurrency can help you assess its security, scalability, and decentralization before staking.

7. Token Economics: The token economics of a cryptocurrency, including its supply dynamics, inflation rate, and distribution model, can impact the long-term value and stability of the coin. Analyzing the tokenomics of a cryptocurrency can help you make an informed decision when choosing a coin for staking.

8. Tax Implications: Staking rewards are considered taxable income in many jurisdictions, so it is essential to understand the tax implications of staking before participating. Consult with a tax professional to ensure compliance with local tax laws when staking cryptocurrencies.

In conclusion, selecting a cryptocurrency for staking requires careful consideration of various factors, including staking rewards, requirements, security, community, liquidity, consensus mechanism, token economics, and tax implications. By conducting thorough research and due diligence, investors can choose a suitable cryptocurrency for staking that aligns with their financial goals and risk tolerance.

- Comparison of popular staking coins and their rewards mechanisms

Staking has become a popular method of earning passive income in the cryptocurrency space. In this section, we will compare some of the most popular staking coins and delve into their unique rewards mechanisms.

1. Ethereum (ETH):
   - Ethereum is in the process of transitioning to a proof-of-stake (PoS) consensus mechanism with the launch of Ethereum 2.0.
   - Stakers on the Ethereum network will be able to earn rewards by locking up their ETH as validators to secure the network.
   - The rewards in Ethereum staking will vary based on factors such as the total amount of ETH staked and network activity.

2. Cardano (ADA):
   - Cardano utilizes a PoS consensus mechanism called Ouroboros, where stakers can delegate their ADA to a stake pool to earn rewards.
   - The rewards in Cardano staking are determined by the amount of ADA staked and the performance of the chosen stake pool.
   - Stakers can earn additional rewards through delegation, which allows smaller holders to participate in the staking process.

3. Tezos (XTZ):
   - Tezos employs a unique PoS mechanism known as Liquid Proof of Stake (LPoS) where users can delegate their XTZ to bakers to validate transactions.
   - Stakers in Tezos can earn rewards through baking or delegating their XTZ, with the rewards being a combination of block rewards and endorsement rewards.
   - The rewards in Tezos staking are distributed based on the amount of XTZ staked and the baking performance.

4. Polkadot (DOT):
   - Polkadot uses a PoS mechanism called Nominated Proof of Stake (NPoS) where users can stake DOT as validators or nominate other validators to earn rewards.
   - Stakers in Polkadot can earn rewards by participating in the staking process as validators or nominators, with rewards being distributed based on the amount of DOT staked and network activity.
   - The rewards in Polkadot staking can also vary based on the performance and reputation of the validators.

5. Solana (SOL):
   - Solana implements a PoS mechanism called Proof of History (PoH) combined with a PoS consensus mechanism to achieve high performance and scalability.
   - Stakers in Solana can earn rewards by delegating their SOL to validators, with rewards being distributed based on the amount of SOL staked and network activity.
   - The rewards in Solana staking are designed to incentivize participation in the network and contribute to its security and decentralization.

In conclusion, staking coins offer a variety of rewards mechanisms that incentivize users to participate in securing and validating blockchain networks. Each staking coin has its unique features and rewards structure, providing stakers with different opportunities to earn passive income based on their preferences and risk tolerance. It is essential for stakers to research and understand the rewards mechanisms of each staking coin before participating in staking activities.

- **Risks and benefits associated with staking different cryptocurrencies**

Staking has become increasingly popular in the world of cryptocurrency as a method for investors to earn passive income by holding and validating transactions on a blockchain network. However, it is important for investors to understand the risks and benefits associated with staking different cryptocurrencies before they decide to participate in this activity.

Risks:
1. Volatility: One of the main risks associated with staking different cryptocurrencies is price volatility. The value of cryptocurrencies can fluctuate significantly, which can impact the overall value of your staked assets.

2. Network Security: Staking involves actively participating in the blockchain network by validating transactions. If the network is not secure, there is a risk of hacks, attacks, and other security vulnerabilities that could lead to the loss of staked assets.

3. Slashing Penalties: Some blockchain networks impose slashing penalties for malicious behavior or failure to perform staking duties properly. This can result in a portion of your staked assets being forfeited as a penalty.

4. Regulatory Risks: The regulatory environment surrounding cryptocurrencies is constantly evolving, and there is a risk that new regulations could impact the legality or profitability of staking activities.

Benefits:
1. Passive Income: Staking allows investors to earn passive income by holding and staking their cryptocurrencies. This can provide a steady stream of income without the need for active trading.

2. Network Participation: By staking cryptocurrencies, investors actively participate in the blockchain network and contribute to its security and decentralization. This can help support the overall health and stability of the network.

3. Inflation Hedge: Some cryptocurrencies use staking as a way to control the token supply and combat inflation. By staking these cryptocurrencies, investors can protect themselves against the devaluation of their assets over time.

4. Potential for Capital Gains: In addition to earning staking rewards, investors may also benefit from potential capital gains if the value of the staked cryptocurrency appreciates over time.

In conclusion, staking different cryptocurrencies can offer both risks and benefits to investors. It is important to carefully consider these factors and conduct thorough research before deciding to participate in staking activities. By understanding the potential risks and rewards, investors can make informed decisions to maximize their returns while mitigating potential downsides.

Chapter 4: Setting Up a Staking Wallet

- Guide on how to set up a staking wallet for storing and managing staked coins

Introduction:
Setting up a staking wallet is a crucial step for individuals looking to participate in cryptocurrency staking. A staking wallet serves as a secure storage solution for your staked coins while also providing the necessary functionality to engage in the staking process effectively. In this guide, we will walk you through the steps required to set up a staking wallet for storing and managing your staked coins.

Step 1: Choosing a Staking Wallet
The first step in setting up a staking wallet is choosing a suitable wallet that supports staking. It is essential to select a wallet that is compatible with the specific cryptocurrency you intend to stake. Popular options include desktop wallets, online wallets, and hardware wallets. Research different wallet options, considering factors such as security features, user interface, and community reviews before making a decision.

Step 2: Downloading and Installing the Wallet
Once you have chosen a staking wallet, the next step is to download and install the wallet software on your device. Visit the official website of the wallet provider to ensure you are downloading the legitimate software version. Follow the installation instructions provided by the wallet provider to set up the wallet on your device.

Step 3: Creating a New Wallet
After installing the wallet software, you will need to create a new wallet within the application. This typically involves setting a strong password and generating a unique set of recovery seed phrases. Ensure you store this information securely

as it will be essential for accessing your staked coins and recovering your wallet in case of any issues.

Step 4: Transferring Coins to Your Staking Wallet
Once your wallet is set up, you will need to transfer the coins you wish to stake into your staking wallet. This process involves sending the coins from your exchange account or another wallet to the staking wallet address provided by your wallet software. Double-check the wallet address before initiating the transfer to prevent any errors.

Step 5: Initiating the Staking Process
With your coins securely stored in your staking wallet, you can now initiate the staking process. Depending on the cryptocurrency and staking mechanism, this may involve simply holding the coins in your wallet or actively participating in the network's staking process. Follow the instructions provided by the wallet software to start staking your coins and earning rewards.

Step 6: Monitoring and Managing Your Staked Coins
Once you have set up your staking wallet and initiated the staking process, it is essential to monitor and manage your staked coins regularly. Stay informed about the staking rewards, network updates, and any changes that may affect your staking activities. Utilize the features provided by your staking wallet to track your staking rewards, manage your staked coins, and make informed decisions about your staking strategy.

Conclusion:
Setting up a staking wallet is a fundamental step for individuals interested in participating in cryptocurrency staking. By following the steps outlined in this guide, you can establish a secure and efficient staking wallet for storing and managing your staked coins. Remember to prioritize security measures, stay informed about the staking process, and actively engage in managing your staked assets to maximize your staking rewards and overall experience.

- Overview of different types of staking wallets (Online, Hardware, Software)

Staking cryptocurrencies has become an increasingly popular method for individuals to earn rewards while contributing to the security and decentralization of blockchain networks. Staking involves holding funds in a cryptocurrency wallet to support the operations of a blockchain network and receive rewards in return. To participate in staking, users need to choose a suitable staking wallet. There are several types of staking wallets available, each with its own set of features and benefits. In this section, we will provide an overview of the different types of staking wallets, including online wallets, hardware wallets, and software wallets.

1. Online Staking Wallets

Online staking wallets, also known as web wallets, are digital wallets that are accessible through a web browser. These wallets are often provided by cryptocurrency exchanges or staking platforms, allowing users to stake their funds directly on the platform. Online staking wallets offer convenience and accessibility, as users can easily access their funds and manage their staking activities online. However, users should be cautious when using online wallets, as they are more susceptible to hacking and security breaches compared to other types of wallets.

2. Hardware Staking Wallets

Hardware staking wallets are physical devices that store users' private keys offline, providing an extra layer of security for their funds. These wallets are considered one of the most secure options for staking cryptocurrencies, as they are not connected to the internet except when making transactions. Hardware wallets typically come in the form of USB devices and require users to confirm transactions manually on the device itself. While hardware wallets offer enhanced security, they can be more expensive than other types of wallets and may require some technical expertise to set up and use.

3. Software Staking Wallets

Software staking wallets are applications or software programs that users can download and install on their computers or mobile devices. These wallets allow users to stake their funds directly from their devices, providing a convenient way to participate in staking activities. Software wallets come in various forms, including desktop wallets, mobile wallets, and browser extensions. They offer a good balance between security and accessibility, allowing users to have more control over their funds compared to online wallets. However, users should ensure they are using reputable software wallets from trusted sources to avoid potential security risks.

Conclusion

Choosing the right staking wallet is an important decision for cryptocurrency holders looking to participate in staking activities. Each type of staking wallet has its own advantages and considerations, depending on factors such as security, convenience, and cost. Online wallets offer accessibility but may have security risks, while hardware wallets provide the highest level of security but come at a higher price. Software wallets strike a balance between security and accessibility, making them a popular choice for many users. Ultimately, users should carefully evaluate their needs and preferences to select the staking wallet that best suits their requirements.

- **Security best practices for protecting staked assets**

Staking cryptocurrency has become increasingly popular as a way to earn passive income by participating in network validation and governance. However, with the potential rewards come risks, as staked assets are vulnerable to various security threats. To safeguard your staked assets, it is crucial to adhere to the following security best practices:

1. Choose a Secure Staking Platform: Before staking your assets, thoroughly research and select a reputable staking platform with a proven track record of security. Ensure that the platform implements robust security measures, such as two-factor authentication (2FA), encryption, and regular security audits.

2. Use a Hardware Wallet: Consider using a hardware wallet to store your staked assets securely offline. Hardware wallets provide an extra layer of protection by keeping your private keys offline and away from potential cyber threats.

3. Secure Your Private Keys: Your private keys are the gateway to your staked assets, so it is essential to keep them secure. Avoid sharing your private keys with anyone and store them in a secure location, preferably offline or in a hardware wallet.

4. Enable Two-Factor Authentication (2FA): Implement 2FA wherever possible to add an extra layer of security to your staking accounts. By requiring a secondary verification method, such as a code sent to your mobile device, you can prevent unauthorized access to your accounts.

5. Regularly Update Software: Keep your staking platform, wallet, and any other related software up to date with the latest security patches. Software updates often include fixes for known vulnerabilities that could be exploited by hackers.

6. Beware of Phishing Attempts: Be cautious of phishing emails, messages, or websites that attempt to trick you into revealing your login credentials or private keys. Always verify the authenticity of communications and only interact with trusted sources.

7. Diversify Your Staked Assets: Consider diversifying your staked assets across multiple platforms or cryptocurrencies to mitigate risk. By spreading your holdings, you can reduce the impact of potential security breaches on a single asset.

8. Monitor Your Accounts Regularly: Stay vigilant and monitor your staking accounts regularly for any suspicious activity. Set up alerts for account logins, transactions, or withdrawals to detect and respond quickly to any security incidents.

9. Secure Your Network: Secure your network connection by using a secure and private internet connection, especially when accessing your staking accounts. Avoid using public Wi-Fi networks or unsecured connections that could expose your sensitive information to hackers.

By following these security best practices, you can minimize the risks associated with staking cryptocurrency and protect your assets from potential security threats. Remember that security is paramount when it comes to safeguarding your staked assets, so always prioritize the implementation of robust security measures.

Chapter 5: Staking Strategies and Tips

- Different staking strategies to maximize returns and minimize risks

Staking cryptocurrency can be a lucrative way to earn passive income, but it is essential to implement the right strategies to maximize returns and minimize risks. Here are some different staking strategies that can help you achieve these objectives:

1. Diversification: One key strategy to minimize risk is to diversify your staking portfolio. By staking multiple cryptocurrencies across different platforms, you can spread out your investment and reduce the impact of any potential losses from a single asset.

2. Long-Term Holding: Staking with a long-term perspective can be beneficial as it allows you to earn more rewards over time. By holding onto your staked assets for an extended period, you can take advantage of compounding returns and potentially increase your overall earnings.

3. Research and Due Diligence: Before choosing a cryptocurrency to stake, it is essential to conduct thorough research and due diligence. Evaluate factors such as the project's credibility, technology, team, market potential, and staking rewards to select assets with strong fundamentals and growth potential.

4. Stake Pooling: Joining a stake pool can help mitigate the risks associated with staking, especially for smaller investors. By pooling your funds with other users, you can collectively stake a larger amount, increasing your chances of earning rewards consistently.

5. Risk Management: Implementing effective risk management strategies is crucial to protect your staked assets. Set clear investment goals, establish stop-

loss orders, and regularly monitor market conditions to adjust your staking strategy accordingly.

6. Reinvestment of Rewards: Reinvesting your staking rewards can accelerate your earnings over time. By compounding your returns, you can increase the size of your staked assets and generate higher passive income in the long run.

7. Staking Ladders: Staking ladders involve staggering your investments across different staking periods to optimize returns and liquidity. By diversifying the duration of your stakes, you can access rewards at regular intervals while maintaining flexibility to adjust your strategy as needed.

8. Dynamic Staking: Dynamic staking strategies involve adjusting your staked assets based on market conditions, project developments, and staking rewards. By staying informed and adapting to changes in the cryptocurrency landscape, you can optimize your returns and mitigate risks effectively.

In conclusion, by employing a combination of these staking strategies, cryptocurrency investors can maximize their returns and minimize risks in the evolving staking landscape. It is essential to stay informed, adapt to market dynamics, and continuously refine your staking approach to achieve long-term success in the world of cryptocurrency staking.

- Tips for successful staking, including timing, network participation, and diversification

Staking has become an increasingly popular method for cryptocurrency holders to earn passive income and actively participate in securing blockchain networks. To maximize your staking rewards and ensure a successful staking experience, it is essential to consider various factors such as timing, network participation, and diversification. Below are some key tips for successful staking in cryptocurrency:

1. Timing is Key: Timing plays a crucial role in staking, as the rewards and staking conditions can vary depending on the cryptocurrency network you are staking on. It is essential to consider factors such as the staking rewards rate, lock-up periods, and overall market conditions before deciding when to start staking. Keeping an eye on network upgrades or changes in staking parameters can also help you make informed decisions about your staking strategy.

2. Active Network Participation: Active participation in the cryptocurrency network you are staking on can enhance your staking rewards and contribute to the overall security and decentralization of the network. This can include voting on governance proposals, running a staking node, or participating in community discussions and events. By staying engaged with the network, you can build a stronger connection with the community and potentially influence network decisions in a positive way.

3. Diversification: Diversifying your staking portfolio across different cryptocurrencies or blockchain networks can help reduce risk and increase your overall staking rewards. By spreading your staking investments across multiple projects, you can mitigate the impact of any potential issues or downtimes on a single network. Additionally, diversification can provide exposure to a wider range of staking opportunities and potentially higher rewards in the long run.

4. Risk Management: Staking in cryptocurrency inherently comes with risks, such as network vulnerabilities, slashing penalties, or market volatility. It is important to carefully assess and manage these risks by conducting thorough research on the projects you are staking on, setting realistic expectations for rewards, and implementing security measures to protect your staked assets. Consider factors such as the project's team, technology, community support, and overall market trends before committing your funds to staking.

5. Stay Informed and Adapt: The cryptocurrency space is constantly evolving, with new projects, technologies, and trends emerging regularly. To stay ahead in

the staking game, it is crucial to stay informed about the latest developments in the industry, network upgrades, and best practices for staking. By continuously educating yourself and adapting your staking strategy to changing market conditions, you can maximize your staking rewards and secure your investments in the long term.

In conclusion, successful staking in cryptocurrency requires a combination of strategic planning, active participation, risk management, and continuous learning. By following these tips and staying proactive in your staking endeavors, you can optimize your staking rewards and contribute to the growth and sustainability of the broader cryptocurrency ecosystem.

- Overview of tools and resources available for stakers to monitor and optimize their staking activities

Staking has become a popular way for cryptocurrency holders to earn passive income by participating in network validation processes. Stakers need access to various tools and resources to effectively monitor and optimize their staking activities. In this section, we will explore some of the key tools and resources available for stakers to enhance their staking experience.

Staking Wallets
Stakers require a secure and user-friendly wallet to store their staked assets and receive staking rewards. Many cryptocurrencies have their own official wallets that support staking. These wallets typically provide features such as staking status updates, reward tracking, and easy access to staking functions.

Staking Platforms
Staking platforms offer stakers the opportunity to delegate their tokens to a validator without needing to run a node themselves. These platforms handle the technical aspects of staking, making it easier for users to participate in staking

and earn rewards. Stakers should choose reputable platforms with a proven track record of security and reliability.

Block Explorers

Block explorers are essential tools for stakers to monitor blockchain activity, track transactions, and verify staking rewards. Stakers can use block explorers to view their staking history, check validator performance, and explore network statistics. Block explorers provide transparency and visibility into the staking process.

Staking Calculators

Staking calculators help stakers estimate their potential earnings based on various factors such as staking amount, staking duration, and network rewards. These tools can assist stakers in making informed decisions about their staking strategy and optimizing their rewards. Staking calculators are valuable resources for planning and forecasting staking activities.

Community Forums and Social Media

Engaging with the staking community through forums, social media platforms, and online discussions can provide stakers with valuable insights, tips, and updates about staking opportunities. Stakers can share experiences, learn from others, and stay informed about the latest developments in the staking ecosystem.

Security Tools

Security is paramount in staking activities, as stakers are required to lock up their funds to participate in network validation. Stakers should use security tools such as hardware wallets, multi-factor authentication, and secure password practices to protect their staked assets from potential threats. Security tools help stakers safeguard their funds and minimize the risk of unauthorized access.

In conclusion, stakers have access to a wide range of tools and resources to monitor and optimize their staking activities. By utilizing these tools effectively, stakers can enhance their staking experience, maximize their rewards, and contribute to the growth and security of the cryptocurrency ecosystem.

Chapter 6: Staking Pool Participation

- Explanation of staking pools and how they work

Staking pools have become a popular option for cryptocurrency holders who wish to participate in staking but may not have the technical expertise, time, or resources to stake on their own. Staking pools allow multiple users to combine their resources and stake collectively, increasing their chances of being chosen to validate transactions and earn rewards. Here is a detailed explanation of staking pools and how they work:

1. Formation of Staking Pools: Staking pools are typically formed by a group of individuals or a dedicated organization that manages the staking process on behalf of the participants. Users interested in staking can join a staking pool by delegating their cryptocurrency holdings to the pool.

2. Delegating Staking Tokens: When a user delegates their staking tokens to a pool, they are essentially transferring the rights to validate transactions and earn staking rewards to the pool operator. However, the ownership of the tokens remains with the user, and they do not lose control over their funds.

3. Increased Staking Power: By pooling their resources together, participants in a staking pool collectively increase their staking power. This enhances their chances of being selected as a validator and earning staking rewards more frequently compared to staking individually.

4. Distribution of Rewards: Staking rewards earned by the pool are distributed among the participants based on their contribution to the pool's staking power. The distribution of rewards is typically proportional to the amount of tokens each participant has delegated to the pool.

5. Pool Operator Fees: In exchange for managing the staking process, pool operators may charge a fee on the staking rewards earned by the participants. This fee is usually a percentage of the total rewards earned by the pool and is deducted before distributing the rewards to the participants.

6. Risk and Security Considerations: While staking pools offer convenience and the opportunity to earn staking rewards without actively managing the process, participants should be aware of the risks involved. It is essential to choose reputable and secure staking pools to mitigate the risk of potential scams or security breaches.

7. Choosing a Staking Pool: When selecting a staking pool, participants should consider factors such as the pool's reputation, performance history, fees, security measures, and transparency. Conducting thorough research and due diligence before delegating tokens to a staking pool is crucial to ensure a positive staking experience.

In summary, staking pools provide a convenient and accessible way for cryptocurrency holders to participate in staking and earn rewards without the need for extensive technical knowledge or resources. By joining a staking pool, users can benefit from increased staking power, regular rewards, and the expertise of pool operators, making staking a more inclusive and rewarding experience for a wider range of participants.

- Pros and cons of joining a staking pool versus staking independently

Staking has become a popular method for earning passive income in the cryptocurrency space. When it comes to staking, individuals have the choice of either joining a staking pool or staking independently. Each option has its own set of advantages and disadvantages, which are important for potential stakers to consider before making a decision.

Pros of Joining a Staking Pool:
1. Lower Entry Barrier: Joining a staking pool typically requires a smaller minimum stake compared to staking independently. This allows individuals with smaller amounts of cryptocurrency to participate in staking and earn rewards.

2. Reduced Technical Complexity: Staking pools often handle the technical aspects of staking, such as maintaining network connectivity, updating software, and securing funds. This can be beneficial for individuals who are not tech-savvy or do not want to deal with the complexities of staking independently.

3. Consistent Rewards: Staking pools combine the staking power of multiple participants, which leads to more frequent and consistent rewards distribution compared to staking independently. This can provide a steady income stream for participants.

Cons of Joining a Staking Pool:
1. Reduced Control: When staking in a pool, participants have less control over their staked funds and the staking process. Pool operators make decisions on behalf of the participants, which may not always align with individual preferences.

2. Fees: Staking pools typically charge a fee for their services, which can eat into the overall staking rewards earned by participants. It is essential to consider these fees when evaluating the profitability of joining a staking pool.

3. Centralization Risk: By pooling resources together, staking pools can potentially centralize the network and concentrate power in the hands of a few operators. This can lead to security risks and reduce the decentralization of the network.

Pros of Staking Independently:

1. Full Control: Staking independently allows individuals to have full control over their staked funds and the staking process. Participants can make decisions based on their preferences and adjust their staking strategy accordingly.

2. No Fees: Staking independently eliminates the need to pay fees to a staking pool operator. This means that participants can maximize their staking rewards without any deductions.

3. Supports Network Decentralization: By staking independently, participants contribute to the decentralization of the network and help maintain its security and integrity.

Cons of Staking Independently:
1. Higher Entry Barrier: Staking independently often requires a larger minimum stake compared to joining a staking pool. This can be a barrier for individuals with limited funds who want to participate in staking.

2. Technical Complexity: Staking independently involves handling various technical aspects, such as setting up a staking node, maintaining network connectivity, and ensuring the security of funds. This can be challenging for individuals without technical expertise.

3. Less Predictable Rewards: Staking independently may lead to less frequent rewards distribution compared to staking in a pool. The variability in rewards can make income generation less predictable for participants.

In conclusion, the decision to join a staking pool or stake independently depends on individual preferences, technical expertise, financial resources, and risk tolerance. It is essential for stakers to weigh the pros and cons of each option carefully before choosing the most suitable staking method for their needs.

- Steps to participate in a staking pool and earn rewards collaboratively

Participating in a staking pool can be a lucrative way to earn passive income through your cryptocurrency holdings. By pooling resources with other users, you can increase your chances of being chosen to validate transactions and earn rewards. Below are detailed steps on how to participate in a staking pool and earn rewards collaboratively:

1. Research Staking Pools: The first step is to research and identify reputable staking pools that support the cryptocurrency you own. Look for pools with a good track record of payouts and security measures.

2. Choose a Staking Pool: Once you have identified a few staking pools, compare their fees, rewards distribution methods, and reputation. Select a pool that aligns with your investment goals and risk tolerance.

3. Join the Staking Pool: To join a staking pool, you will need to follow the specific instructions provided by the pool operator. This usually involves creating an account on their platform and linking your cryptocurrency wallet to the pool.

4. Deposit Cryptocurrency: After joining the staking pool, you will need to deposit your cryptocurrency into the pool's staking wallet. This will be used to stake and validate transactions on the blockchain.

5. Stake Your Cryptocurrency: Once your funds are deposited in the staking pool, they will be combined with other users' funds to increase the chances of being selected to validate transactions. The more cryptocurrency you stake, the higher your potential rewards.

6. Earn Rewards: As part of a staking pool, you will earn rewards based on the

amount of cryptocurrency you have staked and the pool's overall performance. Rewards are typically distributed periodically, either in the form of additional cryptocurrency or a percentage of transaction fees.

7. Monitor and Reinvest: It's important to regularly monitor your staking pool's performance and adjust your staking strategy as needed. Consider reinvesting your earned rewards to compound your earnings over time.

8. Withdraw Rewards: When you are ready to withdraw your rewards, most staking pools will allow you to do so through their platform. You can choose to reinvest your rewards, transfer them to your personal wallet, or convert them to another cryptocurrency.

By following these steps, you can effectively participate in a staking pool and earn rewards collaboratively with other users. Remember to conduct thorough research, choose a reputable staking pool, and stay informed about market trends to maximize your staking rewards.

Conclusion

- Recap of key concepts covered in the book

In this book, several key concepts have been covered to provide readers with a comprehensive understanding of staking in the cryptocurrency space. This section serves as a recap of the essential points discussed throughout the book:

1. Introduction to Staking:
The book begins by introducing readers to the concept of staking in the world of cryptocurrency. Staking involves participating in the validation process of transactions on a blockchain network by locking up a certain amount of cryptocurrency as collateral.

2. Proof of Stake (PoS) Mechanism:

The book delves into the Proof of Stake (PoS) consensus mechanism, which is the underlying protocol that enables staking. PoS allows network participants to validate transactions and create new blocks based on the amount of cryptocurrency they hold and are willing to stake.

3. Staking Rewards:

Readers are introduced to the concept of staking rewards, which are the incentives offered to stakers for actively participating in the validation process. These rewards can vary based on factors such as network participation, staking duration, and overall network performance.

4. Staking Pools:

The book discusses the concept of staking pools, which allow multiple users to pool their resources together to increase their chances of being chosen as validators and earning staking rewards collectively. Staking pools are a popular option for users who may not have enough cryptocurrency to stake individually.

5. Risks and Considerations:

The book also covers the risks and considerations associated with staking, such as the potential for slashing penalties in case of malicious behavior, network downtime, and market volatility. Readers are advised to carefully assess these risks before engaging in staking activities.

6. Staking Wallets and Platforms:

The importance of choosing a secure staking wallet and platform is highlighted in the book. Readers are encouraged to select reputable wallets and platforms that offer robust security features to safeguard their staked assets.

7. Future Trends and Developments:

The book concludes by touching upon future trends and developments in the staking ecosystem, such as the emergence of new PoS-based cryptocurrencies, advancements in staking technology, and regulatory developments that may impact staking practices.

Overall, the book provides readers with a comprehensive overview of staking in the cryptocurrency space, covering key concepts, mechanisms, rewards, risks, and considerations. By understanding these fundamental aspects of staking, readers can make informed decisions when participating in staking activities and navigating the evolving landscape of the cryptocurrency industry.

- Future trends and developments in the staking ecosystem

As the cryptocurrency market continues to evolve, the staking ecosystem is set to experience significant growth and innovation in the coming years. Staking, which involves participants locking up their cryptocurrency to support network operations and earn rewards, has become increasingly popular due to its potential for passive income and network security benefits. Here are some key future trends and developments expected in the staking ecosystem:

1. Expansion of Staking Offerings: With the increasing popularity of staking, we can expect to see a wider range of cryptocurrencies offering staking capabilities. This expansion will provide more options for investors looking to participate in staking activities across different blockchain networks.

2. Enhanced Staking Protocols: Future developments in staking protocols are likely to focus on improving efficiency, security, and user experience. Projects will work on optimizing staking processes, reducing entry barriers, and enhancing user interfaces to make staking more accessible to a broader audience.

3. Interoperability and Cross-Chain Staking: Interoperability solutions will enable stakers to participate across multiple blockchain networks seamlessly. Cross-

www.ingramcontent.com/pod-product-compliance
Lightning Source LLC
Chambersburg PA
CBHW070954220526
45471CB00007B/3025

In addition, staking provides a mechanism for token holders to earn passive income in the form of staking rewards. By staking their tokens, participants can receive regular payouts based on their contribution to network security and consensus. This financial incentive not only rewards users for their support but also encourages them to actively engage in network governance and decision-making processes.

Overall, staking plays a crucial role in the broader cryptocurrency landscape by promoting network security, community participation, market stability, and financial incentives for token holders. As the adoption of staking continues to grow, it is essential for investors and users to understand its benefits and implications for the future of decentralized systems. By embracing staking, stakeholders can contribute to a more secure, inclusive, and prosperous cryptocurrency ecosystem.

technology. Stakers and investors should stay informed about these trends to capitalize on the opportunities presented by the evolving staking landscape.

- Final thoughts on the importance of staking in the broader cryptocurrency landscape

Staking has emerged as a significant aspect of the cryptocurrency ecosystem, offering a unique way for token holders to participate in network maintenance and governance while earning rewards. As the blockchain industry continues to evolve, staking is playing an increasingly crucial role in shaping the future of decentralized systems.

One of the key benefits of staking is its role in securing blockchain networks. By staking their tokens, participants contribute to the validation and verification of transactions, thereby enhancing the overall security and integrity of the network. This decentralized approach to consensus mechanisms, such as proof of stake, helps prevent centralization and ensures a more democratic and resilient network.

Moreover, staking also promotes network participation and engagement among token holders. Unlike traditional mining, which requires expensive hardware and technical expertise, staking is a more accessible and environmentally friendly way for users to support blockchain networks. This inclusivity encourages broader community involvement and fosters a sense of ownership and responsibility among stakeholders.

Furthermore, staking can incentivize long-term holding and reduce market volatility. By locking up their tokens for staking, investors are less likely to engage in speculative trading or panic selling, which can lead to price fluctuations. This stability benefits both token holders and the overall health of the cryptocurrency market, creating a more sustainable and robust ecosystem.

chain staking platforms and bridges will facilitate the movement of assets between different blockchains, allowing stakers to diversify their holdings and maximize rewards.

4. Decentralized Staking Pools: Decentralized staking pools will offer stakers the opportunity to pool their resources with other participants, increasing their chances of earning rewards. These pools will operate in a trustless manner, ensuring transparency and security for all stakeholders involved.

5. Staking Derivatives and Financial Products: The emergence of staking derivatives and financial products will provide stakers with additional opportunities to hedge risks and optimize returns. Products such as staking derivatives, staking-as-a-service, and yield farming strategies will allow stakers to leverage their assets and earn additional income.

6. Governance and Participation Incentives: Projects will focus on enhancing governance mechanisms within staking networks to empower token holders and promote active participation. Incentive programs, voting mechanisms, and community engagement initiatives will encourage stakers to contribute to network decision-making and maintenance.

7. Environmental Sustainability: With growing concerns about the environmental impact of blockchain networks, staking projects will explore more energy-efficient consensus mechanisms and sustainability initiatives. Proof-of-Stake (PoS) networks will continue to gain traction as a greener alternative to energy-intensive Proof-of-Work (PoW) systems.

In conclusion, the future of the staking ecosystem is poised for significant growth and innovation. With a focus on expanding offerings, improving protocols, fostering interoperability, and promoting sustainability, staking is set to play a vital role in shaping the future of decentralized finance and blockchain